MW01593496

Combat and Capture

The Memoirs of Flight Officer
Claude W. McCrocklin
1941 - 1945

by

Claude McCrocklin and
Mark Armstrong

INFINITY
PUBLISHING.COM

Copyright © 2009
by Claude McCrocklin and Mark Armstrong

*All rights reserved. No part of this book shall be repro-
duced or transmitted in any form or by any means, elec-
tronic, mechanical, magnetic, photographic including pho-
tocopying, recording or by any information storage and re-
trieval system, without prior written permission of the
publisher. No patent liability is assumed with respect to
the use of the information contained herein. Although
every precaution has been taken in the preparation of this
book, the publisher and author assume no responsibility for
errors or omissions. Neither is any liability assumed for
damages resulting from the use of the information contained herein.*

ISBN 0-7414-5491-2

Published by:

INFIN∞ITY
PUBLISHING.COM

1094 New DeHaven Street, Suite 100
West Conshohocken, PA 19428-2713
Info@buybooksontheweb.com
www.buybooksontheweb.com
Toll-free (877) BUY BOOK
Local Phone (610) 941-9999
Fax (610) 941-9959

Printed in the United States of America

Published August 2009

Contents

Foreword...i

Chapter I 1
    Enlistment and Training 2

Chapter II...6
    Monte Cassino Abbey - 15 March, 1944.......................6
    Crisis over Vienna, Austria - 17 March, 1944................7
    Klagenfurt, Austria - 19 March, 1944 8
    Bologna, Italy Strike - 22 March, 1944 8
    Snow Storm over the Alps - 26 March, 1944 9
    Combat and Capture – Part 1 9

Chapter III...14
    Combat and Capture – Part two 14

Chapter IV 20
    Combat and Capture – Part Three 20

Chapter V 30

Chapter V 30
    Stalag Luft I Prison Camp – Part 1 30
    Seeing the other Side of the War 32
    Adjusting to Life as a Prisoner of War 35
    Camp Routine 36
    Food 38
    Close Calls 39
    Uncertain Times 41

Chapter VI 44
    The Russians...44
    Summary...49

Chapter VII..50
    It was not all bad – Some Humorous............................50
    Incidents..50
    Chewing Gum...50
    The Cigars...50

The Cookies 51
The Errol Flynn Episode 52
Ham and Eggs 53
Soap and Razor 54
The Button 55
Wahoo 56
The Photograph 57

Conclusion 59

References 61

Appendix A - A Stalag Luft 1 Christmas At Barth,
      Germany 1944 62

Appendix B - War Status of the Flight Crew of "Miss
      Zeke" A/C #42-52276 64

Appendix C - Claude W. McCrocklin - Fact sheet 66

Appendix D - Excerpt from a speech given to the
      Centenary College R.O.T.C (Reserve
      Officer Training Corp) students: 67

Illustrations – Pictures

Cover – Prisoner of War Medal depicting a winged eagle
      surrounded by barbed wire

Page 4 – Claude McCrocklin upon graduation from flight
      school

Page 5 – Flight crew of *Miss Zeke*

Page 7 – *Miss Zeke* over Monte Cassino

Page 18 – Claude McCrocklin in parachute after plane was
      shot down

Page 25 – Interrogation

Page 29 – Arrival at Barth, Germany

Page 31 – German Identification card for Claude McCrocklin

Page 66 – Warren Stuckey and Claude McCrocklin

Foreword

Four-mile Creek, fall – 1936 Southwest Arkansas

Closely following a squirrel high above, Claude watched as it jumped from the main trunk of a tree to a high branch and stopped, twitching its tail. Leveling his .22 caliber rifle, he aimed carefully and squeezed the trigger. He felt the report, and saw the squirrel fall onto the forest floor.

Looking for a path to where the squirrel had fallen, he noticed he had wandered into a nest of water moccasins. Surrounded by several snakes, Claude stood perfectly still as the snakes began hissing and taking on a defensive posture, all ready to strike.

Although scared, he calmly reloaded the single-shot rifle. Without bringing the rifle to his shoulder, he lowered it near the closest snake he was facing and pulled the trigger. At the same instant, he leaped over and ran.

For many years, this was the nightmare that he awoke to in the middle of the night. That is, until the world was at war and he left home to fight for his country.

He would live through many experiences that would, and did, replace the nightmares of his youth. Although only twenty-three at war's end, he wasn't a youth at all. He was an experienced combat veteran; a veteran of thirteen air missions over Europe at the height of the air war.

The majority of this memoir has been posted on a couple of web sites for a number of years. When revising the text for typographical errors, I decided it was time to pull everything together for better flow, to include a number of stories that were not posted to the web sites, or were too hidden to notice, and to provide a brief background for those with limited historical knowledge of World War II.

Claude's original text and wording have been left alone. They are well written and record how he wishes to share his experiences during the War. Being his nephew, there are more stories I can and have provided the reader regarding family history. Especially where related to Claude or where they may help the reader better understand his background.

This information is provided to the reader at the beginning of each chapter, where needed, and through footnotes. The web site chapter titles have been left intact and will serve the reader as indicators that Claude's original text follows.

I have attended a number of presentations where Claude has shared his war experience with groups of people. At each presentation, without fail, he tells a story I've heard previously in a different way, adding a little more to what I know of his experience during the war.

I am the only person in my family that has not been in the military. This, I feel, is from the sacrifices made by Claude and his generation. I write this in part for my respect of an Uncle and for the next generation to understand those sacrifices made by so many.

Mark D. Armstrong

Bossier City, LA
December 2008

Chapter I

Claude Walter McCrocklin was born on January 15, 1921 near Fouke, Arkansas and was the eldest of three brothers and one sister. His father was employed in the oil field that required the family to move every few years over a four state area (Kansas, Arkansas, Texas and Louisiana). Most of his childhood was spent on his grandfather's farm in southwest Arkansas at a place called Sylvernio, a community just north of Fouke and a little south of Texarkana, Arkansas. It was here that Claude learned to hunt, fish, and, involuntarily, farm.

His high school years were spent in a town in east Texas named Overton. Being a little over six-foot in height with an athletic build, Claude excelled in sports. He was an all-star fullback on the football team when it was time for his father to move once again and follow the booming oil field, Claude decided to remain in Overton and finish high school staying with the coach's family.

Claude was in Overton at the time of the New London school explosion on March 18, 1937 and was one of many athletes recruited to go the school to help. New London was a few miles from Overton when on the afternoon of the 18th, a gas explosion ripped through the school killing around 300 students, teachers, and workers. Upon arrival, the Overton athletes were fortunately turned away by men working the gruesome catastrophe. What he briefly viewed would haunt him for a number of years to come.

Upon graduation from Overton, he received a scholarship in football and began classes in 1940 at Centenary College in Shreveport, Louisiana.

Claude's immediate family and ancestors have fought in a number of wars for the United States. His father was in the Army during the Philippine-American War 1899/1913 and served through World War I. It was through his father that Claude knew of life as a foot soldier during war that helped in his decision to join the Air Corp.

His Great-Grandfather fought for the Confederacy and was captured at Battle of Port Hudson. He was interred at the Union Prisoner of War camp Johnson's Island in Ohio throughout the remainder of the War. Claude heard recounts at an early age, of life as a prisoner of war. In some of his presentations, he mentions that he was carrying on family tradition by becoming a prisoner of war himself.

Another notation that should be made is that during World War II, the Army Air Corp was manned solely by volunteers. It had strict guidelines for enlistment and a rigorous training program. At any time should an enlistee fail, they would be transferred to the regular service. Many volunteers did not succeed.

After training, the crews assembled at Davis Montham Army Air Base in Tucson, Arizona for crew assignments. It was at this base that each crew was assigned to a plane. The flight crews were chosen by superior officers. However, a Pilot could replace a crew member with one of his choice if he desired to. Claude persuaded the Pilot, William Terrell, to replace a crew member with a childhood friend, Warren Stuckey, after being asked to do so by Warren's sister whom Claude had dated before attending college. Warren's sister was certain that if her brother were with Claude, he would safely return home after the war.

Enlistment and Training

In 1941-42 I was a student at Centenary College. I was on a football scholarship and trying to get an education. On December 7, 1941, I was out with a date who was also a Centenary student and who would later become my wife. War was the last thing on my mind, I had not even thought of it, but all of that changed overnight when the Japanese bombed Pearl Harbor[1] and we were at war. It would be to-

---

[1] Claude later learned that his first cousin Hubert Aaron was killed on the battleship Arizona during the attack.

day like the Russians bombing Miami, or New York.[2] Things changed overnight at Centenary. Campus life and all of those things that seemed so important yesterday now were overshadowed by war. Every male student knew that he would be in the military soon. The only choice was to either wait or be drafted, or to enlist. I chose to enlist, because there was to me a certain stigma in having to be drafted when your country was in danger. I visited the Army, Navy and Marine Corp recruiting offices to see which service I wanted to fight the war with. Without hesitation I volunteered for the Army Air Corp. It was to me the most adventurous and exciting way to fight the enemy. I took my physical and written examinations at Barksdale Army Air Base[3], as it was called then, and was accepted as an aviation cadet. I was called to active duty in 1942 and sent to California for pre-flight school. I wanted to be a fighter pilot, but upon graduation, was classified as a bombardier.[4] As a bombardier cadet I was sent to Advanced Bombardier School at Deming Air Force Base in Deming, New Mexico where I learned how to use the Norden bombsight and finally got into an airplane[5].

---

[2] The memoir was written in the middle 1980's when the Cold War was still a reality.

[3] Now known as Barksdale Air Force Base located in Bossier City, LA.

[4] Claude also tells of a story where upon learning he was chosen to be a bombardier instead of a fighter pilot. He confronted the officer in charge of the placement and was told they needed bombardiers and not fighter pilots at the time, and, if he did not like the choice he could join the regular Army.

[5] Claude was trained in a Beechcraft AT-10

The Norden bombsight was one of World War II's top secret weapons, and each bombardier had to take an oath to defend it with his life, if need be. A Norden bombsight can be seen today on display at the Louisiana State Museum at the fairgrounds.[6]

Upon completion of Advanced Bombardier School, I was commissioned a Flight Officer in the Army Air Corp, and assigned to a B-24[7] bomber crew. After several months of training at various B-24 bases, our crew was assigned to the 744th Squadron, 456th Bomb Group, and 701st Wing of the 15th Air Force in Italy[8]. We flew the B-24 to Italy via Brazil, the South Atlantic Ocean, North Africa and the Mediterranean Sea.[9]

Right-Claude McCrocklin upon graduation from Flight School.

---

[6] The museum is located in Shreveport, Louisiana.

[7] Claude flew in a Consolidated B24 J Liberator aircraft.

[8] The airbase was located near the city of Cerignola, Italy.

[9] There was no in-flight refueling at that time. Planes were either ferried on ship by sea (normally fighter planes due to their small size) or were flown to their station from base to base such as Claude's plane.

Above photo taken at Charleston AFB in December of 1943

1st row (left to right) Flight Officer Seymor Stutzel, Navigator; Lt. William R. Terrell, Pilot; Lt. Phillip L. Crum, Copilot; Flight Officer Claude W. McCrocklin, Bombardier

2nd row, standing (left to right) Sgt. Charles W. Doerring, Nose Gunner; Sgt. Palmer P. Lerum, Tail Gunner; Sgt. Dennis D. King, Top Turret Gunner; Sgt. Herman Lipkin, Radio Operator/Left Waist Gunner; Sgt. Chester H. Eide Jr., Ball Turret Gunner; Sgt. Warren Stuckey, Right Waist Gunner

Chapter II

Claude reached the base in Italy in early March 1944 and began his experience in World War II Europe. His memoir only recounts fully his thirteenth and final mission but he did record a few other missions in another "recollection" which will be included here before the narrative of his final mission.

Monte Cassino Abbey - 15 March, 1944

I was in one of the 36 456th BG B-24J's that led this important bombing raid on Monte Cassino. Our Squadron was in the lead element of the formation so I had a clear view of the action. Cassino Abbey was on the top of a snow covered mountain that was the most important fortress in the German line across Italy that was blocking the Allied advance up the Italian peninsula. All efforts by ground troops to take it were repulsed with heavy losses, so the 15th Air Force was called in to take it out. Since the Abbey was a Catholic Church, this decision was made with reluctance, but was paramount to save not only Allied casualties, but to keep the Germans from pushing the Anzio beachhead back into the sea.

Once we got the order to destroy Cassino, 500 LB GP (general purpose) demolition bombs were used to destroy it and the Germans on top of the mountain. The day of the mission was cold and clear. Cassino was a perfect target as I picked up in my bombsight. Just as I was finalizing the drop, a flak burst near the front of the plane broke my plexiglass window in front of the bombsight and shattered glass hit my face. This, plus the rush of sub zero air hitting me; momentarily dazed me to the extent that I no longer could use the bombsight, so I "salvoed" (dropped the bombs all at once), four tons of high explosives on the Abbey. The result of this near getting killed on the bomb run made me realize for the first time that flying combat was no "fun and game" sort of thing and a man could get killed doing it!

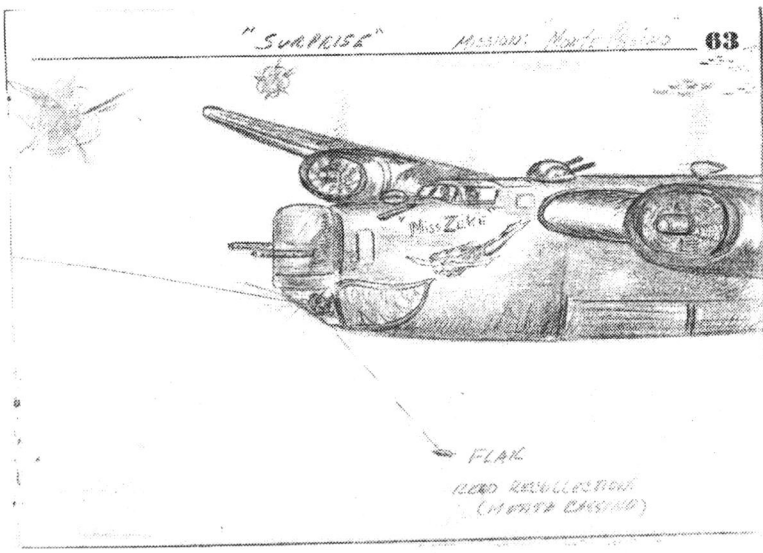

"Miss Zeke" sketch from Claude's Wartime Journal

Crisis over Vienna, Austria - 17 March, 1944

One of the seldom mentioned hazards of WWII flying over Europe was the intense cold at 20,000 to 25,000 foot altitude. Since none of the planes had pressurized cabins all were open to the cold. The crew was protected by electric wired flying suits, but the plane's equipment was exposed and often froze up including the bombsight. This happened to my Norden bombsight and bomb bay compartment on this mission.

With a frozen bombsight and bomb bay doors that would not open, I as the bombardier had to take off my parachute and flak jacket and go back to the bomb bay, crank open the doors and release the bombs manually with a screw driver. This was no easy task standing on a narrow catwalk holding on with one hand and leaning over and tripping each bomb's release. This was a very hazardous experience and I still dream of it!

On this same mission one of the waist gunner's fifty caliber guns jammed. The gunner, without thinking, took off his electric heated glove to clear it. When his bare hand touched the cold metal it froze to it and he had to stand there with his hand stuck on the gun until we could descend to a warmer temperature so his hand could thaw out. He was lucky to still have a hand when we got back to Italy.

The recorded temperature inside the plane that day was 42 degrees below zero!

Klagenfurt, Austria - 19 March, 1944

Shot down our first German fighter plane on this mission. It was an ME109 that was sent up to radio our air speed, altitude and direction to flak guns below so they could zero in on the B-24's. He was so absorbed in his mission that he got in too close. I watched our red tracer bullets hit his plane causing instant disintegration of both him and his ME109. I watched it go down and explode near a farm house. My feeling was not exultation of having shot an enemy plane down, but why he was so stupid to fly in so close. I can still see him in the cockpit as those fifty caliber bullets hit him. It was not a pretty sight to remember.

Bologna, Italy Strike - 22 March, 1944

I first saw the devastating effect of mass bombing on this mission. Our target was the railroad yards and station of Bologna. It was a sunny day with clear visibility. As our flight turned on the bomb run course I picked up the target with my Norden bombsight and placed the cross hairs square on the rail road station and trains. The place was jammed with people of all ages. Through the bombsight telescope I saw faces of the people as they looked up at the planes and impending bombs. I for some reason looked square in the faces of a little boy and his mother! I will never forget the look of terror on their faces. As the bombs hit, they and entire trains were exploded causing great carnage. I was shaken then and am now by the memory of that little boy and his mother. I am not proud that I was a bombardier, because a bombardier kills people whole sale as at Bologna, Italy!

Snow Storm over the Alps - 26 March, 1944

Enemy action was not the only hazard flying over wintertime Europe. On this mission into central Europe we ran into an intense cold front with zero visibility. The entire Air Force got lost and scattered over Southern Europe. We would occasionally break out into an open space in the clouds and could see for a few minutes what was around us. As I was in the plexi-glass nose compartment of the plane I could see everything. It was an eerie feeling watching the snowflakes hit the plexi-glass as I watched for enemy fighters. One time as the clouds opened a flight of twelve German FW190 fighters were on our wing tip! They were also lost. We saw each other about the same time, but before either of us could react we were back in the clouds.

We finally let down below the clouds and saw the Adriatic Sea and flew south down the Italian Coast arriving at our base after dark and low on gas. We were lucky to have made it back!

Combat and Capture – Part 1

Air war in Europe during 1943 and for the first six months of 1944 was a bloody business. The German Luftwaffe[10] had air superiority over the target areas in Central Europe at the time, because our fighters did not have the range to escort the bombers all the way to the target. Our losses consequently were heavy. The average number of

---

[10] Luftwaffe translates into English as Air Force.

missions in my group was two. This meant that on your second mission you were likely to be shot down. Some never even got to the target. We were told that our mission at that stage of the war was to knock out the German Air Force in the air and on the ground. The theory was, we can replace our losses, and they cannot, so we slugged it out. My military rating in addition to the bombardier was "observer." This meant that during the flight to and from the target, I observed and wrote down everything that happened. Many times I counted up to 20 B-24's and B-17's[11] shot down on a single mission. Since each one had a ten-man crew[12], you can imagine what the casualty rate was. And, since we were always hundreds of miles behind enemy lines, every plane that went down was a total loss.

A major World War II bombing mission in Europe was an awesome sight. It would involve anywhere from 500 to 1,000 planes. Can you imagine today what it would be like to see that many planes in the air at one time? The world never again will see such a sight. Just to get that many planes off the ground and into formation was quite an achievement. I will try to describe it to you: A World War II bomber Squadron consisted of six or more planes with a minimum of six Squadrons to a Group, and three Groups to a Wing. There were then several Wings to an Air Force. All of these planes would line up on the runways and take off at 20-second intervals, then fly around until they got into formation in groups of 36 planes. When they all finally got together, the air force would be strung out for miles in an irregular "stacked up and down" formation. High above the bomber formations would be our fighter cover which would stay with us until we reached the limit of their range, or they were attacked by the enemy. Either way, when they left, we

---

[11] B-17 refers to a Boeing model 17 "Flying Fortress."

[12] A crew consisted of a Pilot, Co-Pilot, Bombardier, Navigator which were all officers and enlisted men in the positions of nose gunner, tail gunner, waist gunners (left and right), bottom "turret" gunner, and top "turret" gunner.

were on our own. The enemy usually attacked the bomber formations at this time. Their object was to break up the formation, scatter the planes, and then shoot them down at will. A favorite tactic was to use their fighter-bombers such as the JU-88[13] to fly just out of range of our 50-calibre machine guns and fire rockets into a formation. While this was going on, several hundred ME-109's and FW-190's[14] would attack at close quarters from every direction. They would fly right through our formation so close you could see the pilot and the instrument panel of his plane. My battle station was in a Plexiglas compartment in the nose of the B-24, which gave me a super view of the entire action. There would be the bomber formation stretched out as far as the eye could see with swarms of enemy fighters attacking from every direction. In addition, to the fighters there were clouds of flak[15] which we had to fly through. As the result of this prolonged close quarter air battle, there would be a stream of debris from exploding and burning planes streaming back through the formations. Men and parachutes would fill the sky. If the chute was white, it was one of ours; if it was yellow, it was one of theirs. No one shot at a man in a parachute, or at a disabled plane with its wheels down, which was a sign of surrender. I have seen disabled German fighters with wheels down fly up beside our planes, the pilot blow his canopy, climb out on the wing and bail out. We watched, but held our fire, because we knew that our time would come and that we would be at the mercy of German pilots. I am alive today because the Germans honored our unwritten code.

---

[13] The Junkers 88 (JU-88) was a German fighter-bomber plane.

[14] The Messershmitt 109 (ME-109) and the Focke-Wulf 190 (FW-190) were German fighter planes.

[15] Nickname given by Allied Airmen for the German anti-aircraft weapon *Flugabwehrkanone* or aircraft defense cannon. The cannon sent large diameter shells into the air which would burst into black clouds and send metal shrapnel in a 360 degree pattern.

The most enemy fighters that we were briefed to meet on any of the missions that I flew was 750. This meant that 750 fighters would hit us on the way in, go down and refuel, then be back up to attack us on the way back. The mission that proved to be the last I flew was to bomb a ball bearing factory at Steyr, Austria, 600 miles north of Italy.

This maximum mission by the 15th Air Force was coordinated with the 8th Air Force's first daylight bombing of Berlin. The object was to divide the Luftwaffe and thus reduce the fighter opposition. It was my thirteenth and last combat action in World War II. The date was April 2, 1944. I had beaten the odds and had completed twelve missions. Of the 36 plus planes that were in my group when I started, only two were left, mine and one more. After this mission, none were left of the original group. There was a complete turnover in 29 days.

Preparations for the mission started at 0400 with a quick breakfast and then off to pre-mission briefing. At the briefing, we were told what the target was. There was a large map of Europe on the wall with a red string leading from our base to the target. We were told the distance to the target, what altitude to fly and what opposition to expect. After this general briefing for all crew members, the lead bombardiers[16] had a special briefing. In this meeting, the bombardiers were given a photograph of the target area and how to find the specific target. We were also given the necessary information such as altitude of the target above sea level, wind direction and velocity, air and ground speed, etc. From this information we could calculate the data to put into the bombsight. Basic data was computed on the ground, the rest of it had to be done in flight which was no easy task with someone shooting at you.

---

[16] The term lead-bombardier was given to the bombardier located in the lead plane of the bomber formation. Bombs were dropped from the other planes in the group based upon when the lead bombardier dropped his.

After briefing, we were taken to the flight line and our plane. The first thing that I did on arrival at the plane was to check the bomb load, particularly the fuses on each bomb to be sure they would detonate on impact. Remember, the object of the bombing mission was to destroy the target. The bombardier was responsible for this, so he had to do his job, otherwise the mission was a failure and many lives lost for nothing. Everything, the preparation on the ground, the battles in the air to just reach the target, all was designed to put the bombardier over the target so he could do his job. After being sure that the bomb load was okay, I then entered the plane and went to my station in the nose compartment. The bombsight and bomb release systems were checked and data previously computed was put into the sight. During the flight, I would make corrections as conditions changed. After checking the plane's equipment, I checked my own. My parachute was missing! I remembered that I was not supposed to fly that day and had put it in for repack.[17] I though a minute and decided that I had flown twelve combat missions and probably would not need it, then too, the plane had already taxied out to the runway and I didn't want to hold things up. An overpowering feeling came over me to get that chute, so I called the pilot on the intercom and told him the situation. He called on the plane's radio for a jeep to take me to the parachute repack station. When I got there, my chute was not ready, so I started to leave without it, when the repack girl said, "Lieutenant, take this extra chute, you might need it". She threw it to me as I was going out the door. She saved my life with that chute as the following events will testify.[18]

---

[17] Claude had been relieved of duty for the day by the flight surgeon due to a head cold. He was "volunteered" for duty by the flight officer who was short on experienced lead bombardiers.

[18] The "girl" was a member of the WAC (Women Auxiliary Corp).

Chapter III

Combat and Capture – Part two

To get to the target that day, our flight plan was to fly across the Adriatic Sea, Yugoslavia, and on into Austria. It was while approaching the Yugoslav coast that we received our first attack. I observed about 50 ME-109 fighters coming in from 11:00 o'clock high[19] and another group of 40 attacking our fighter escort, who were still with us at the time. This initial attack scattered our escort and forced them to drop their extra fuel tanks. This meant that we were on our own for the rest of the day. Since it was only about 0830, we would be over enemy territory under constant attack for the next six to seven hours. I personally saw up to 21 B-24's shot down before we reached the target area. There were many others that I could not see, but knew what was happening from the large number of parachutes in the air.

On this mission I was deputy lead bombardier.[20] My squadron of planes led the Air Force. We flew in "boxes" of six planes, at a minimum, and in "V" formation so close to each other the wings almost touched. This was done for mutual protection and to get the desired bomb pattern on the target. On reaching the target area, there was an intense barrage of flak that covered the area and swarms of every kind of German fighter they could put in the air. We made it to

---

[19] Airmen during World War II utilized the face of a watch or clock to reference enemy attacks. The reference would be made as though the plane were at the center of a clock face. An 11 o'clock attack would be from directly above and slightly to the left of the plane. Conversely, if an attack came from the 5 o'clock position, it would come from directly below and slightly to the right.

[20] Deputy Lead Bombardier meant that Claude was second in position behind the Lead Bombardier.

the IP[21] and turned on the bomb heading. I had five minutes to find the target, pick it up in the bombsight and make final adjustments. The plane had to be level when the bombs went out, otherwise you missed. I flew the plane with the bombsight during this period.[22] My main concern was to find the target. They did not draw a "bull's-eye" and thus say, "Here it is". Unless you were bombing a city, or railroad which could not be missed, the target was always heavily camouflaged.

On this occasion, there had been a heavy snowfall which made the camouflaged target even more difficult to pick up at 22,000-foot altitude. I constantly checked the photo taken by our scout plane the day before and given to me at the briefing before the mission. From the photograph, I followed the bends of the Steyr River to the target and finally identified it about three minutes before the bombs would have to be released. During this final three minutes, the 15th Air Force lead plane directly in front of our plane took a direct hit and exploded. We pulled up in its place and took over the lead. While this was taking place, 20-mm shells from two ME-110[23] fighters on our tail began to explode in the plane, killing or wounding one half of the crew and one engine began to burn. All of this in three minute's time! Since our plane was now leading the air force, and all remaining planes on our group would drop their bombs when mine were released, I had to concentrate on the target. At 30 seconds before the bombsight would release the bombs, which had yellow streamers on them as a signal for all planes to drop theirs, I finally synchronized and thus locked the

---

[21] IP is the acronym for Initial Point. Bomb Squadrons would fly a certain direction before turning on their bomb run. This would keep the enemy guessing what the target was until the last possible moment.

[22] For maximum accuracy during the bomb run the plane was flown by the Bombardier using the Norden bombsight.

[23] The Messershmitt BF-110 (erroneously noted by WWII Airmen as an ME-110) was a fighter-bomber.

computer[24] on target. This meant nothing short of the plane exploding could prevent hitting the target. On release of the bombs, I watched them go down to the target. On impact the camouflage was blown away and the target laid bare for the more than 500 planes behind us to home in on. My feeling at the time was one of satisfaction and pride for having successfully done my job. This feeling of exultation did not last but a moment, because the next pass of the ME-110's knocked out another one of our engines and killed our top turret gunner who was about four feet behind and above me. I was talking to him and suddenly he was hit by a direct burst of 20-mm cannon fire. Blood gushed all over everything. I had been too busy concentrating on the bomb run to be scared before. Now I was terrified with the sudden realization that I too would likely be killed. This felling passed as I was busy directing the two remaining gun turrets.

With two engines gone, we had to fall out of formation and fly back to Italy alone. We got as far as Zagreb, Yugoslavia, where we were attacked by six ME-109 fighters. I watched them take off from Zagreb Air Base, circle and climb high above us. We had two gun turrets still operational, the bottom ball turret and the nose turret, which was directly in front of me. Our top, tail and both side gunners had either been killed, or seriously wounded. Any attack from above, rear, or side could not be stopped.

Consequently, the six ME-109's attacked from the top and rear in flights of two. I watched from a Plexiglas observation bubble on top of the plane[25]. It is strange how in what you think are your last moments you can remember so vividly. The ME-109's were painted blue gray, they had yellow, black and white markings and the pilots wore blue uniforms

---

[24] The computer being referred to is the Norden Bombsight – an analog computer.

[25] The small Plexiglas bubble was located in front of the cockpit and just behind the nose of the plane and was primarily used for navigation.

with black helmets. As they passed within thirty feet or so of our plane, I could even see the expressions on their faces!

An ME-109 had six 30-calibre machine guns in the wings and one 20-mm cannon firing through the propeller hub. We survived their first attack, but the second one started us burning so badly we had to bail out. I pulled my flak jacket release string letting it fall to the floor of the plane, put on my chute, opened the nose wheel door and prepared to jump. The altimeter said 10,000 feet, the time was 1330[26] hours.

I looked at the strange snow covered landscape below and jumped. The leg strap of my parachute hung on the nose wheel door and I could not get clear. After much struggling, I climbed back into the plane and jumped the second time. I pulled the rip cord when I was clear of the plane, but was tumbling end over end and when the canopy partially opened. I was wrapped in the shroud lines, but managed to get them sorted out. The first sensation was how quiet it was after the noise of the air battle. I watched two more of our crew bail out and the six ME-109's finish off our plane which was still on auto pilot and trailing fire and smoke. I watched fascinated as it crashed and exploded in a huge column of fire. The ME-109's, their work finished, circled and one peeled off and headed directly toward me. I was scared, because I thought that he was coming to shoot me in the parachute. I reached up and pulled one side of the chute's shroud lines, thus partially spilling the air out so that I could fall fast and he couldn't get a bead on me. This was a foolish thing to do, because I almost couldn't stop my fall. I finally managed to get air back into the canopy and the chute working again. The ME-109 was still with me. This time I resigned myself to the worst and just stared at him. He flew in real close, looked over at me, smiled and saluted! Later, I would meet him on the ground and hear him tell me, "All I

---

[26] Military time is noted in twenty-four hour periods. 1330 is 1:30 PM.

was doing was following you down and radioing your position to our soldiers so they could pick you up!"

I landed in a tree top which bent over and slung me into a snow bank which cushioned the fall. I still hit so hard it stunned me. My parachute never functioned properly. The tree and snow bank probably saved my life. It is very difficult to get out of a disabled plane under attack. It is nothing like the sky divers you see on TV. After I collected my senses, I took stock of my situation. I was dazed, extremely fatigued and had an intense thirst. My lips were cracked and bleeding, my tongue stuck to the roof of my mouth and trying to eat snow burned, it would not melt. This dehydration was caused by breathing pure oxygen in the plane for five or six hours. I saw a small stream nearby and headed for it. The water helped immensely and I was able to eat two Benzedrine tablets from my escape kit. The "pep pills" gave me a "lift" and brought my senses back. I then started

Sketch from Claude's wartime journal

to plan my escape. The first thing I did was bury the chute in the snow, so (as I thought) the enemy couldn't find it. I then looked around and saw a small church and some buildings in the distance. Since I was in Yugoslavia where the people were supposed to be friendly, I reasoned that I could get help there. I was mistaken. They would have nothing to do with me and ran me off. This was a shock, but later understood when I found out that they would have been shot if they had helped.

After this I started South across an open field to get to a forest on the other side. It was heavy going in two feet of snow. My heavy flying gear made it worst, and the ME-109 was back! He buzzed me so low I could have hit him with a snowball. I no longer considered him a danger, having realized if he had wanted to kill me he could have done so long ago. About this time I heard the command "Halt!" I froze, looked around and saw nothing, so I took another step and heard, "Halt!" once again. This time I put my hands up, and when I did, German soldiers got up all around me with guns at ready. I had not seen them because of the snow cover. One came forward and searched me while the others stood back. They had already found my parachute which is not surprising since I had left a trail in the snow wherever I went. I had lost my pistol in bailing out, but would not have tried to shoot it out with them anyhow. An airman on the ground is no match for infantry soldiers who are trained for just such a situation. For me, the war was over and another phase of my life was to begin.

vailed, or I would not be writing this today. I was shaken; it had been a narrow escape from death. It is one thing to face death in combat, but quite another matter when you are helpless.

Shortly after this, while I was still shaken up, I had another encounter of a different kind. The ME-109 pilot, who had shot me down and buzzed me in the parachute, sent for me. He had been shot down himself later that same day and had parachuted into the same area. When he had found out that I was there and of my narrow escape with the SS, he sent for me. I spent all afternoon visiting with him in the officer's quarters, which was quite a change from the stable. He as a 1st Lieutenant in the Luftwaffe, was about 21 years old, and spoke perfect English. He was friendly, but serious minded and did not try to interrogate me. We talked about the war only in general terms and mostly about air battles in which we had both participated in. I was given food, wine and cigarettes and had regained my confidence lost during the previous encounter with the SS. All of this lasted until the army officers came back from patrol. They were furious at the Luftwaffe lieutenant for bringing me into their quarters and called the guards to throw me back into the stable.

Four days later I was taken to the Luftwaffe base in Zagreb. I was now a prisoner of the German Air Force and treatment improved immediately, I do not know if the ME-109 pilot brought about the transfer, but always felt that he did. In World War II the German P.O.W. camps were operated by the different branches of the armed forces. If you were Air Force, you were prisoners of their Air Force, the Luftwaffe. If you were an Army P.O.W., then you were sent to one of their army camps, etc.

From Zagreb, Yugoslavia, I was taken by train first to Vienna, Austria, and then to the Luftwaffe's main interrogation center, Dulag Luft[30] at Frankfurt, Germany. I had an interesting experience in Vienna. Our train was late arriving and we missed the train to Frankfurt. This meant that we had almost a whole day's layover in Vienna. The two Luftwaffe guards did not want to sit in the train and "guard" me all day, so we all went to a large serviceman's canteen (USO) which was operated by the German Red Cross. On arrival, we found the place packed with every kind of soldier in the armed forces. It was with difficulty that the Luftwaffe guards got us a table. I was fascinated with the sight of so many enemy soldiers in such a relaxed casual manner. Here were the Nazis super soldiers that I had been told were so fanatical in battle. There were SS Panzer men in black uniforms, the Wehrmacht[31] in field gray, the Kriegsmarine (Navy) and Luftwaffe in blue. They were laughing and talking like any soldier on leave. The Red Cross girls in their red and white "waitress" type uniforms were busy serving food and refreshments. The music in the background made the war seem far away. Here I was sitting dressed in my U.S. Army flying uniform with all of its insignia in plain sight and no one said a nasty word to me, or tried to kill me!

After getting over the initial psychological shock of being there in such surrounding, I noticed that there was an SS Panzer tank crew sitting at the table next to mine. They were different from the other soldiers; they never smiled and had cold hard faces. I decided to try and talk to them, because I was curious to learn more about these elite soldiers who had made the word "blitzkrieg"[32] synonymous with mechanized warfare. There was an empty chair at their table so I went over and asked if I could sit down.

---

[30] Dulag Luft is short for **durchgangslag**er luft or transit camp for airmen. Dulags were established in Germany and occupied countries as interrogation centers.

[31] In English this translates as Armed Forces – Army.

[32] In English this translates as "lightning war."

Their crew captain looked me over with cold blue eyes and said, "Why?" Not knowing what to say otherwise, I said, "I am curious about your black uniforms with the silver skull and cross bones insignia on your berets. What do you do?" He told me that he and his crew were on leave from the eastern front where they had been fighting my "friends" the Russians. He asked me did I know what they did to captured German prisoners. I told him I had never seen a Russian, much less knew what they did. I quickly told him how well the German P.O.W.'s in America were treated and most of them were former tank crews from Rommel's Afrika Corp. This "cooled" the situation and we visited and drank "ersatz"[33] coffee. During the whole time, no one smiled or changed their expression. I found out what I wanted to know, "Do not mess around with the SS". They had no sense of humor and were a cold, hard lot.

We finally left Vienna and started the long train ride to Frankfurt. Since we were traveling by day coach, I could observe the people and countryside. I thus saw the "other side" of the war and Germany while they were still strong and powerful. There had been few daylight bombings of Germany by Americans and I was more of an object of curiosity than of hatred in April, 1944. On arrival in Frankfurt, I was quickly taken to Dulag Luft interrogation prison for captured air officers. Here I was put into solitary confinement. It was a very small "closet" type cell with a bright light burning continuously. There was a slot in the door where once a day a bowl of soup and two slices of bread came through. I saw no one and lost all sense of time. To keep from going nuts, I did all sorts of things like counting the cracks in the wall, or bugs in the straw mattress. I finally thought of tapping on the wall (in Morse code) to see if I could contact anyone. I tapped out "May Day", the airman's distress call. I was startled when the reply came back, "I am a South African pilot, who are you?" He was a P-40 pilot who was shot down and

---

[33] In English this translates as "substitute."

captured in Italy. With someone to communicate with, it was not as bad as it was and my morale picked up immensely.

I am not sure just how long I was in solitary, but it was several days. Suddenly I was taken out and into a large lavishly furnished room where well-dressed people were sitting around drinking cocktails and listening to music. A girl in an evening dress came over, smiled and said in perfect English, "Lieutenant would you like a drink and a cigarette?" I was embarrassed, it had now been about two weeks since I was shot down and I had not had a chance to bathe, brush my teeth, or shave. My uniform was dirty and crumpled and I felt like I looked. I realized that the whole thing was designed to humiliate and soften me up for interrogation. It backfired, instead my initial embarrassment turned to anger and I was more determined than ever to resist. I looked her in the eye and said, "American officers do not accept favors from the enemy, leave me alone!" When I said this, a Luftwaffe officer

Sketch from Claude's wartime journal depicting his interrogation

came in and made me stand at attention before a large desk within the same room. He sat behind the desk and proceeded to interrogate me.

The first thing that he did was pull out a large file on me and my military unit in Italy. He first told me where my home was in the states, my parent's names, my father's occupation and his company's name, where I received my education and where I enlisted in the Air Force. He then told me where my air base was in Italy, my squadron and group number and my base commander's name! I was amazed, all the things that I was determined not to give him, he already knew! Thoughts raced through my mind such as, why was I important enough to the enemy that they would go to so much trouble to keep a file on me before I was captured! I found out after the war that the Luftwaffe did this on all air officers whom they thought would be in positions of importance in our air force. They knew that if we flew against them long enough that there was a great possibility that sooner or later we would be shot down.

When he finished reading my history to me, he asked the question, "What was the serial number of your plane?" I did not know, because we changed planes so often. I answered with my name, rank and serial number. He replied, "If I give you the first and last numbers will you fill in the rest?" Since I did not know anyway, I gave the first numbers that came into my mind. He then chided me by saying, "It is rather stupid of you not to even know your plan's number, let me give it to you!" He held up a large photograph of my plane with the serial number clearly visible. I knew it was my plane, because of the squadron and group markings. Since I saw the plane crash and burn after I had bailed out, I knew that the photo had to have been taken in Italy!

I will not go into all of the interrogation that followed. I will just say that all he got out of me was my name, rank and serial number. He finally got mad and threatened me with the SS who he said used "Japanese methods" to get information out of P.O.W.'s When this did not work either, he called the guards, the interrogation was over. I was taken out in the hall, stripped of my uniform and left standing. I didn't know what this was for, but if they wanted to humiliate me, they succeeded. It is hard to keep your dignity while standing naked in a busy hallway. Eventually I was brought an old British uniform that was too small and taken outside jam-packed with Anglo-American air P.O.W.'s. Many of the P.O.W.'s were badly wounded or severely burned. Two German officers in immaculate uniforms were walking among the wounded. When I asked one what they were doing, he said in effect, "We are researching the type of wounds; we get valuable information on how to treat our own wounded that way." I thought it was ironic that seriously wounded P.O.W.'s could help the enemy that way.

Shortly after this I was given a cardboard-suitcase-type Red Cross clothing package which contained a toothbrush, comb, soap, razor, shaving stick, gloves, sweater and flannel pajamas! I was elated! For the first time in nearly three weeks, I could brush my teeth, wash, shave and comb my hair. It was a terrific morale boost and I was in much better spirits. I didn't have much time to enjoy this unexpected windfall, because the Germans soon hustled me and all the other P.O.W.'s to attention. The enlisted men were separated from the officers and were sent to a different camp. The rest of us, about eighty-five officers, were lined up and formed into five squads with German NCO's as squad leaders.

We then marched off to a waiting train, which was to take us to the permanent Luftwaffe camp Stalag Luft I[34] at

---

[34] Stalag is short for Stammlager. Stammlager Luft 1 literally translates into Air Base Camp 1. In World War II, captured Allied soldiers and airmen became the responsibility of the armed force of their counterpart. Hence, captured Allied airmen became the responsibility of the German Air Force (Luftwaffe – Air Force). As mentioned in the text, they were also separated by rank with officers and enlisted men being kept in separate camps.

Barth, Germany. Barth is about ninety miles northwest of Berlin on the Baltic Sea coast. During the long train ride from Frankfurt, many escape schemes were plotted by the P.O.W.'s, but all were thwarted by the fact that our guards took our shoes and dog tags (identification tags). We were told if we succeeded in escaping from the train and were caught without our dog tags, we would be shot as spies. Then too, the prospect of jumping out of the train barefooted into the snow cooled even the most fervent desire to escape.

The most exciting event of this trip was an air raid while we were in the Berlin railway yards. It was an unusual experience to be on the ground and a target of our own planes. I thought how ironic to be killed by our own bombs. Lucky for us they missed our train. I had bombed trains in Italy and knew what could have happened to us. I remember one particular mission to the city of Bologna in northern Italy where we caught the railway yards full of trains, passenger as well as military. The result was carnage. I still remember the expressions of terror on the people's faces as they saw the bombs falling. Now I was on the receiving end and knew how they felt. It is not a pleasant feeling regardless of the politics of war.

After five cold and sleepless nights on the prison train, we arrived at Barth and Stalag Luft I where I would stay the next fourteen months. At six the following morning, our shoes were returned to us and we were routed out of the train by steel helmeted guards. After a silent two-hour march through the fog and drizzling rain, we arrived at the camp. High barbed wired loomed before us behind which were low wooden barracks. The first thing we did on arrival was go through the processing procedure for new prisoners. This consisted of being assigned a P.O.W. number, filling out an I.D. Card and having our picture taken. I was now "Kriegsgefangenen[35] No. 4211".

---

[35] Translates into prisoner of war

The next thing was to be herded into a square brick building and told to remove all our clothing which were tossed into large cauldrons to be deloused. The Germans were fastidiously clean and took every precaution to prevent any outbreak of typhus caused by lice. While our clothes were being deloused, we were given a bar of soap and lined up for showers. We had two minutes of hot water and one minute of cold. Brief as it was, it was great. It was good to be clean again after nearly a month without a bath! After the shower, our clothes were returned and after dressing we were taken to the inner gates and led into the camp itself. On our way we got our first glimpse of the other prisoners. There

were thousands of them. Being shot down and captured seemed a unique experience and it was a surprise that it should happen to so many others as well. I had felt that becoming a P.O.W., like getting killed, always happened to someone else, an unreal experience.

Sketch from Claude's wartime journal depicting arrival at Barth, Germany

Chapter V

Stalag Luft I Prison Camp – Part 1

I was a prisoner of war at Stalag Luft I located at Barth, Germany, from April, 1944, through May, 1945. While in the camp I kept a wartime log of events that happened and illustrated many of them with colored drawings. The wartime log book was supplied by the War Prisoners Aid of the YMCA and its contents are the research material for this memoir. In addition to the wartime log material, I obtained photographs and material from German files while with the Russians who overran and liberated Stalag Luft I before Germany surrendered.

I do not attempt to tell all that happened, for to do so would require the writing of a larger book. Neither do I discuss the politics, or overall strategy of the war. I only tell of some of my experiences and views. At the time these events took place, I was 22 years old, about the age that most young men graduate from college and start out in life. In my case it was different. I had been through so much by the time I got home in late 1945 that it took several years to adjust to "normal" life. I never did quite make it, because the qualities that make a first-rate combat soldier are quite different from those of ordinary men and hard to explain. I am proud that I had those qualities and would do the same thing again if necessary.

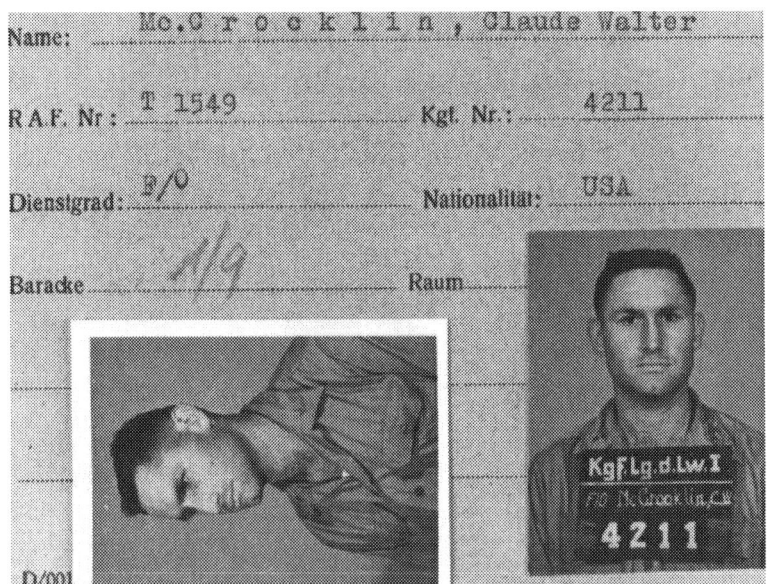

Name:	Mc.C r o c k l i n , Claude Walter
R.A.F. Nr:	T 1549
Kgf. Nr.:	4211
Dienstgrad:	P/O
Nationalität:	USA
Baracke	1/9
Raum	
D/001	

German Photo Identification Card taken on arrival at
Stalag Luft 1

Stalag Luft I in German the name means "Air Prison Camp No. 1". As the name implies, it was a prison camp for captured allied airmen, mostly British and American. At its peak in 1944 it contained 10,000 prisoners of war. Since it was designed to hold only about 2,500, it was very crowded with some of the newcomers being housed in tents. The camp was located on a small peninsula of the Baltic Sea coast on about the same latitude as Hudson Bay in Canada. It got very cold in the winter and even the short summers were cool. The camp was only 60 miles across the Baltic from Sweden, but might as well have been 1,000 miles as far as any escape attempt across it. When I arrived in April, 1944, there were some British RAF (Royal Air Force) officers there who were captured in 1939. No one in the six years that the camp was operated made a successful escape. Getting out of the camp was hard enough, but the hundreds of miles of hostile country to travel just to reach friendly territory were insurmountable.

The camp was run by the German Luftwaffe (Air Force) with an "Oberst" (full Colonel) in charge of administration. He and his staff had full responsibility for the overall camp operation, but they were checked periodically by both the Gestapo[36] and SS who was the political wing of the Nazi armed forces.

In addition to the Germans, there was another authority in the camp to which the prisoners of war were subject. This was the allied command with the senior allied prisoner of war in charge. Even though you were a prisoner of war in an enemy prison, you were still an officer in the U.S. Air Force and expected to act accordingly. All combat air officers in World War II were briefed on how to act if captured and what the U.S. Government expected of you. It was called, "The P.O.W. Code of Ethics". I knew of no one in Stalag Luft I who violated the code.

Stalag Luft I was perhaps the best of the Luftwaffe officer camps and I was fortunate to be there, yet it was by no means a picnic. It was nothing like the sixties TV series, "Hogan's Heroes" where the Germans were cast as "bumbling nitwits" and the prisoners did mostly as they pleased. Colonel Hogan and his cohorts would have been shot in the real world of a prisoner of war camp.

Seeing the other Side of the War

Upon arrival at Stalag Luft I it was a great surprise to see how big it was. There were row upon row of long wooden barracks and thousands of prisoners of war. All of the prisoners of war were officers and there was only one to four on each plane. Since less than 40% of the airmen shot down survived, that meant that the Luftwaffe was shooting down an awful lot of our airplanes! To further boggle the mind, Stalag Luft I was only one of many prisoner of war camps

---

[36] Gestapo is short for Geheime Staatspolizei and translates into Secret State Police.

operated by the Luftwaffe. The camp nearest to ours was Stalag Luft III which had as many, or more, prisoners of war as we did. I knew that we had been taking a beating in the air war in 1943-1944, but this seemed ridiculous. After the war, I read that the total number of allied planes shot down by the Luftwaffe was 85,000! I remember that during the peak of the air war in Europe in 1943-1944, we were told that our losses were "light" and that the Luftwaffe's was heavy. Now I was on the "other side" of the war as a prisoner and could see the contrast between what I had been told and the reality of things. It was a discouraging way to start life as a prisoner of war.

While in the camp, the prisoners had access to German magazines and newspapers. The barracks had speakers in them through which German radio broadcasts were piped in. The programs were usually the broadcasts to the German people and not directed to the P.O.W.'s in particular. The music was good, especially since I liked "polkas" and if you could understand German, the news broadcasts, even though one sided, helped to keep up with the war. The most interesting radio broadcast I heard in World War II was the final one by Radio Berlin in May 1945. It was a "play by play" description of the fall of Berlin to the Russians. The announcer stayed on the air and narrated the attack on the radio station. It went like this: "I see the Russian infantry and tanks coming down the street, I hear the infantry in the building, they are in the hall, the door is kicked in open..." Then I heard shots and after this, silence. Radio Berlin was off the air. Before he was killed at the microphone, this German announcer made one prophetic statement which has stuck with me all of these years, it was: "Germany has fought a good fight. We were the first western nation to recognize and fight the threat of international communism and alone faced the Red Terror. Instead of helping us defend the west; our Anglo-American brothers joined the communists and fought against us. Now that Germany is defeated, the Anglo-Americans will find that their ally, the communists, will turn against them and they will have to face them alone", I will let you come to your own conclusion based on world events today, 40 years later.

While a prisoner of war, I listened to German, Russian and British propaganda, and yes, American, before and after I was captured. I came to the conclusion that at least 50% of it was just as the word implies, "propaganda". It was interesting, though, to hear and compare. For instance, before I was captured, I was told how cruel the Germans were and that I as a bombardier would most likely be treated badly. None of this happened to me. Instead, I was treated according to the rules of the Geneva Convention for the treatment of prisoners of war. To me this was a surprise, especially after I saw the amount of death and destruction caused by our bombing of cities on the train ride through Yugoslavia, Austria and Germany. To the German civilians, allied airmen were "terror flyers" and the war criminals of World War II. If Germany had won, we would have been tried and convicted at Nuremberg. I did not fell guilty about the bombing, but it was still disturbing to the mind to see the results of it. While I was flying missions, there was only one mission that I questioned. It was a bombing raid on the city of Vienna.

We were told at the bombardier briefing that the mission was political and the object of it was to kill as many Austrians as possible to weaken their morale. The target was a residential district and we coolly selected the various types of bombs to kill the most people. The first wave of planes would carry demolition bombs to tear things up, the second wave would carry incendiary bombs to set it on fire and the third wave would drop fragmentation bombs to kill the people when fire drove them out of their shelters. Later, as a prisoner of war, I was taken to Vienna and saw the results of that bombing. As I was led through the crowds of angry people who were shouting all sorts of bad things at me such as "murderer" and "killer of babies," the guards told me to look down and not to say anything. They said that it was their duty to protect me, but that they would not kill their own people to do it. I got the message and acted accordingly.

Another incident in Yugoslavia made me acutely aware of how enemy people felt about American flyers. I was locked up in a room with a large window facing the sidewalk on a busy street. The people would come by, look in and shout insults. Mothers would bring their children to see the "terror flyer." They would spit on the window and make faces at me. I felt for the entire world like a caged animal on exhibit. The guards were not aware of what was going on since they were inside the building. I did not call them, because I was in no physical danger. Instead of feeling humiliated, I was fascinated with the hostile attitude of the people and with my change of status in life. After I arrived at Stalag Luft I, I learned that many airmen who were captured by civilians were treated badly. I was fortunate not to have parachuted down into one of those bombed cities and captured by civilians. It would be like the Russian Air Force destroying my home town of Shreveport and killing 10,000 or more people, then one bailing out over the city and you got your hands on him. What would you do?

I tell of these things so maybe you can understand how I felt, first as a combat flyer and then as a war captive. It is quite a contrast and requires a psychological adjustment. I hope that you never have the experience.

Adjusting to Life as a Prisoner of War

I do not pretend to speak for all prisoners of war in World War II, or the wars that followed. I can only tell my views and how I coped with it. First and foremost, you must be able to adjust to the radical change in your status. The day before your capture you were a person of importance, you were free and honored by your country. Suddenly you are in the hands of the enemy who despises you and would as soon kill you as not. It is quite a shock. Do you remember the expressions on the faces of the captured pilots in the photos that came out of Hanoi during the Vietnam War? This is what I mean.

I was able to make the adjustment by rationalizing my situation. I realized that although I was unlucky enough to be shot down and captured, it could have been worse, I could have been killed, or badly wounded as many others were. I did not allow myself to "hate" the enemy, because hatred consumes you and causes you to act irrational. I did not "like" the Germans, but neither could I ignore them. To help me survive and to increase my changes of escaping, I learned enough German to understand what they were saying and to communicate. I was thankful that I did, because being able to communicate saved my life on several occasions while a prisoner of war. It is my opinion that Russian or Chinese should be taught in our schools today instead of so much French and Spanish. My high school Spanish was useless to communicate with a German-speaking enemy.

Camp Routine

The everyday life in the camp can best be described as repetitious. It was as dull and boring as the individual prisoner of war made it. Personal attitude made the difference. If it was positive and on the upbeat, things were generally okay, but if you lapsed into feeling sorry for yourself it was miserable. I took things one day at a time and tried to make the most of that one day. I planned ahead on how I would react if certain things happened, but realized that my options were limited as a P.O.W. and did not let it bother me.

We had many things to keep us busy in the camp. There were two roll calls daily, one in the morning and one each evening. The roll calls, though routine, could be quite an adventure when we tried to mess them up to cover an escape attempt. The Germans would usually tolerate one, or two miscounts, but if we persisted in screwing up the count, they would bring up the machine guns, fix bayonets and say,

"Now we will get an accurate count, will you please cooperate?" We would get the message and cooperate.

Playing games occupied a lot of our time. Not athletic games such as baseball, volleyball, etc. These burned up needed calories, but parlor games such as chess, bridge and cribbage. We also had a library, mostly British books that had passed the German censor. I enjoyed the ones about the British mountain climbing expeditions to Mount Everest and read them over and over. We also had a theater and a camp orchestra where on occasion talented prisoners of war turned actors would put on vaudeville-type shows. Occasionally, an old film would be shown. I watched Richard Dix in the movie "The Iron Horse" so many times that I memorized it. Time could be passed in other ways depending upon the talents of the individual. I sketched pictures of camp life and drew portraits with colored pencils and water colors supplied by the Red Cross. The greatest pastime of all was watching our planes come over! One time, it felt as though the entire 8th Air Force made a low level pass over Stalag Luft I. They were so low that we could see crew members waving at us. The sound of the engines was like thunder. It was glorious! Tears come in my eyes today when I think of the sight and remember how it lifted our morale during those dark days of the winter of 1944-1945. God only knows how I would have liked to have been with them! As I watched them until they disappeared over the horizon, I felt for the first time the full impact of frustration and despair that marks the life of a prisoner of war in an alien and hostile land. I hope that none of you ever have to experience it.

We also watched the German planes. There was an air base near the camp and we would watch them take off and land. Since they were flying against the Russians on the eastern front, by timing them, we could tell about where the front was. We also watched air battles over and around the camp. You could tell by the sound of the guns who was shooting the most. One time a B-17 was shot out of formation and was limping back to England. It got as far as Stalag

Luft I and the nearby air base when it was shot down by ME-109's. Four of the crew bailed out and we watched them float down. One landed just outside the camp and was picked up by our guards. He was lucky, for we found out later that the other three were captured and beaten to death by civilians.

Food

Two things were paramount on each prisoner of war's mind: food and the progress of the war. Contrary to what you might think, thoughts of home and girlfriends occupied very little of our thinking and conversation. When you were hungry and trying to survive, you think of the present. Food was the big thing. It came from two sources, the German rations and the Red Cross food parcels. If either one was missing, we went hungry. When we had the Red Cross parcels to supplement the German ration of black bread, turnips, cabbage, potatoes or barley, we had enough. Not all that we wanted, but enough to maintain our health. When for various reasons the Red Cross food parcels stopped, or the German rations were cut, we were in trouble. In January, February and March of 1945, we were not only very short of food, but water as well. The heavy bombing of the German railroads and of the water works in the nearby town which supplied our camp, virtually stopped all supplies from reaching us. The absence of enough water hurt the most, because you get used to hunger, but never to thirst. For the first time I felt the effects of malnutrition. I would black out and have to hold on to something to keep from falling if I got up too quick while sitting or lying down. This dark period was the low point of my confinement and I had some doubts as to whether I would ever get out of that place. Even though I felt rather low myself, I tried not to show it, because someone had to be the "cheerleader". Many of the men looked to me as a leader and would come for encouragement. Some would come with their will written out on scraps of paper and say, "Take this back to my family, I don't think that I will make it", etc. I did the best I could to help them and since none of them committed suicide by running out and trying to climb the fence as some did, I know that I succeeded.

Close Calls

A favorite pastime at Stalag Luft I was planning escape attempts. It was a dangerous game with people often getting killed in the process. No one ever made it, but Germans expected it and we felt it our duty to keep trying. The favorite method and the most hazardous were digging tunnels. The tunnels were long and narrow and sometimes collapsed on those digging them. Several times we had to call the Germans to rescue P.O.W.'s trapped in a "secret" tunnel before they suffocated. I did not like tunnels anyhow, because I had claustrophobia, so I thought of other ways to try to escape. One attempt was planned with two other men. The plan was to make wire cutters out of ice skate blades and since snow was on the ground, white smocks out of bed sheets for camouflage. The plan was to hide out in the wash house the evening before the actual attempt to see if I could avoid detection, especially by the guard dogs which roamed the camp at night. I hid in the wash house and watched the guards lock up the barracks. Everything went well until later other guards came around to check the wash house. I just had time to pull myself up on a rafter out of reach of the dogs, (which were vicious wolf-size brutes) when the guards flashed a light on me and told me to put up my hands, or they would shoot. I had a big problem, if I let go of the rafter to put my hands up, I would fall into the dogs. If I didn't, I would be shot! I was very thankful that I could speak enough German to reason with them, because these guards spoke no English. I told them to call off the dogs and I would gladly put up my hands. This they did and were quite satisfied with themselves for thwarting an escape attempt. This experience was not without its humor, for I now know how a treed possum feels.

Another time that I risked being shot was my own fault. I had planted a small garden in an out-of-the-way place and had sat down beside it day dreaming and did not notice how late it was. Barth, Germany is so far north that in summer it stays twilight until about 11:00 p.m. The barracks had already been locked up and I couldn't get in. Since any P.O.W. outside at night could be shot on sight, I had to think of something quick. I knew it was just a matter of time before dogs discovered me. The problem was to let the guards know where I was without being shot in the process. I decided upon a direct approach. At least it would be over quickly. I stood up with my hands in the air and shouted in German, "Nichts schiesen, ich bin heir, machen zie das kaserne offen bitte."[37] Pandemonium broke loose, search lights zeroed in on me, guards and dogs came running and needless to say, I was the center of attention. Once again, knowing the enemy's language and being able to communicate probably saved my life.

In the summer of 1944, the Germans decided to allow P.O.W.'s who would sign a parole to have a day of freedom outside the camp. Everyone took advantage of the opportunity. Since we were on a peninsula with water on three sides, we were still relatively contained, but a P.O.W. on parole would not try to escape anyhow. In the first place, the Germans could shoot you for violating the parole, and second, if you were successful in getting back to your own army, you would be sent back to the Germans. You could, however, while out on parole size up the countryside for future escape routes. This we did.

When the day came to be paroled we were let out in small groups with each man going where he pleased. It was great to be out in the countryside away from the dull, drab prison camp. The smell of the pine forest, the green grass and beautiful flowers and an occasional sight of a deer were wonderful. I had wandered well back into the forest when

---

[37] Translated as "Do not shoot, I am here. Please open the camp gates."

suddenly topping a ridge found myself in the midst of a company of German infantry soldiers on the other side. They were in full battle dress and were on a training mission in the forest. It was a tense moment. Had they been told that there were P.O.W.'s on parole in the area? I did not know, but had to react quickly and in a positive manner. I had on a U.S. Army uniform with a huge "KGF" sign in red across the back of my jacket. The "KGF" letters were an abbreviation for Prisoner of War in German.[38] There was no doubt who I was, but did they think that I had escaped and needed to be "recaptured"? I decided to act normal and as if nothing unusual was happening. I walked on down among them, smiled and said, "Gut morgan soldaten, haben zie em gut tag," which meant "Good morning soldiers, have a good day". They were as surprised as I was and some smiled and waved back. They were young, mostly teenage and looked for all the world like a group of R.O.T.C. Cadets in summer training, which they probably were. I was their first glimpse of the "enemy". I wondered what their thoughts were.

Uncertain Times

In March and April of 1945 the collapse of Nazi Germany was imminent. The Russians were advancing rapidly from the east and the Anglo-Americans from the west. Germany was moving the prisoner of war camps ahead of the advancing allied armies, especially in the east. Stalag Luft III at Sagan had already been evacuated with the prisoners forced to march west into the German heartland. It was a terrible hardship and ordeal for the P.O.W.'s. We were in no physical shape to make forced marches in the cold and snow. Then, too, Hitler had ordered all captured enemy air officers to be killed. I have a copy of that order in my files today to remind me of the reality of those times. Stalag Luft I at Barth was the only major P.O.W. war camp in the east that had not been moved. The Luftwaffe colonel in charge of our camp

---

[38] Kriegsgefangenen or Prisoner Of War

refused to obey Hitler's orders to move, or kill us. To help him decide to disregard Hitler's orders, our planes came over and dropped leaflets on the camp and surrounding area. The leaflets had a photo of Roosevelt, Churchill and Stalin and said that the Germans at the camp and in the area would be held personally responsible for our safety.

During these uncertain times, our allied P.O.W. command decided to form a secret P.O.W. commando unit to resist the Germans long enough to allow most of the P.O.W.'s to escape if Hitler's orders to kill us were attempted. The commando unit was called the "Field Force" and it was not only to provide protection for the P.O.W.'s as stated above, but to make contact with the advancing Russians. Out of the 10,000 P.O.W.'s in the camp, 100 were selected. I was one of those men. The first that I knew of it was when a courier came and told me to report to the P.O.W. commander's office. Upon arrival, I was told to go to a certain room in another barracks for a meeting. At this meeting I was told of the Field Force and that I had been chosen to be part of it. I was told that such an organization within the camp was illegal and had to be top secret. I was also told that if we were discovered we would most likely be shot, but not to let that bother me, because we would all be killed anyway if we had to fight the Germans to give time for the bulk of the P.O.W.'s to escape. This did not bother me at all, because I had been "volunteered" for suicide missions before and by this late stage of the war had so many close brushes with sudden death that it now seemed the "normal" way of life. I was in fact eager to get a gun in my hands once more and have a chance to fight again. I had been a P.O.W. for ten months at the time and was tired of just "sitting" helplessly and watching the war go by.

We met secretly during March and April, made our plans and familiarized ourselves with the German weapons, then waited. Nothing happened until one morning during the last week of April, 1945. We woke up and found the German guards gone! They had abandoned the camp and retreated deeper into Germany. We knew that the Russians were near, but where? Did they know about us, or would they take Stalag Luft I as a German installation and attack? We had to contact them as quickly as possible. Until we did, all P.O.W.'s were ordered to stay in camp. Field Force men were put in the guard towers to warn everyone not to leave the camp. We could not have 10,000 ex-P.O.W.'s roaming the countryside in the face of the Russian army. The Russians might think that they were Germans and open fire. After this danger was explained, the men stayed put in the camp and Field Force units were sent out to contact the Red Army.

Chapter VI

The Russians

My first impression of the Red Army was negative. It was a mixture of curiosity and disappointment. The Russian infantry was made up of all ages of men and women, young boys who looked 15 or 16, and men in their fifties. About every fourth or fifth one was a woman. Later after the war when I read that the German army had killed 10,000,000 Russian soldiers, I knew why they looked as they did; they were "scraping" the bottom of the barrel!

Most of their equipment was "make shift" and American lend-lease. Their uniforms were a mixture of American G.I.[39] shirts worn with the tails out and Russian army pants and boots. The whole thing was kept together by a belt around the waist. Only the officers and elite units had good equipment and sharp looking uniforms. I was also surprised as the many ethnic groups: Ukrainians, Turkomens, Armenians, Mongols and, of course, Russians, to name a few. The Russian soldiers were as a whole boisterous and unpredictable. The junior officers and non-com's[40] were a surly lot and distrusted us. It did not matter that we were also officers of an allied country; only the senior Russian officers recognized this and acted accordingly.

As a member of the Field Force, I was issued a pass by the Russian commander which allowed me to move freely among the army and to go where I wished. I was given an arm band to identify me to the Russian soldiers and assigned to a guard unit positioned on the perimeter of the town. This allowed me to observe all that went on and to have close contact with the soldiers. I, as a result, got to know well

---

[39] Acronym for Government Issue
[40] Short for Non-Commissioned Officer usually refers to sergeants.

Russian mentality and behavior. I did not like what I saw. All communist armies were brutal and savage, especially toward helpless people under their power. I felt sorry for the German civilians, especially for the refugees who had fled before the advancing Russian army and now were caught by them. I could tell of many atrocities committed by the Russian army while I was with them, but will only tell of two that I prevented.

The Russians had put a large group of German women and children in an open field without food, water, or shelter, and ordered them to stay there. At the time that I saw them, they had already been there a day or two and were very hungry and thirsty. I went to the P.O.W. camp, where a surplus of Red Cross food parcels were stored and got all of the food and water that I could carry in my field bag. I then returned to the field and walked out among the people. At first they were afraid of me, thinking that I was Russian, but when I spoke to them in German and told them who I was, they wept for joy. It broke my heart to see such needless suffering, especially of the children. I passed out what food and water I had and told them that I would get more and return tomorrow. At this time, a Russian non-com and a squad of soldiers arrived and told me to quit wasting food on Germans and to get out of the field. I showed him my pass signed by his commander, which said, among other things, that I was free to go where I pleased. This was a tense situation that had a happy ending. The Russians left and I told the people that they could find shelter in an abandoned military school building across town where other refugees were staying. As I turned to walk away, a little blond, blue-eyed girl about five years old ran up and held on to my leg. She looked up and said, "Danke gut mann", which meant, "thank you good man". It was all of the thanks that I needed. I picked her up and hugged her and said that I wished that I could do more. As I walked away with tears in my eyes, I disliked the Russians even more.

In another incident, my dislike for Russians turned to outright disgust. Women of all ages were regarded as war "booty" and were treated accordingly. Many mothers would kill their children and themselves before they could be captured by the Russian soldiers. Even though I had become hardened to the sight and smell of death by 1945, I could not get used to seeing dead women and children lying in the fields around the town where they had gone out and shot themselves. They did this to escape what they considered a fate worse than death...falling into the hands of the Russians!

To illustrate why many German women felt as they did about Russians, I will tell of one incident in which I was directly involved through no fault of my own.

I was on sentry duty with a Russian unit and was on an outpost. I heard in the distance women screaming and crying. When I could make out what was going on, I saw a Russian sergeant with a squad of soldiers herding a croup of teenage German girls along the sentry line and passing them out to each soldier on duty. When they got to me he had two left. He, very business like checked his list until he came to my name, crossed it off and threw the girls down at my feet. He then grinned, made an obscene gesture, and left, his "duty" over. I was dumbfounded! I looked down at the girls who could not have been over fifteen or sixteen years old lying face down in the dirt crying. When I got my sense together I said in German, "I am an American officer. Please stand up and tell me your name and where you live, when I get off duty I will take you home". I will never forget the look of relief and hope in their eyes when they looked up on hearing their language and the assurance in my voice. They sat by the sentry post until my relief arrived. I escorted both to the older girl's home and on arriving was impressed with the beautiful house and cultured, well-educated family. I was embarrassed by the deep-felt expressions of gratitude expressed by the mother and grandmother. I looked the family over and noticed one old man and two young children in addition to the mother and grandmother. I asked where the men of the family were. The mother said that her son was killed early in the war and her husband was missing on the eastern front. I stayed a little while longer and then got up to leave. When I did, they all said, "please don't leave, if you do the Russians will come back, as long as you are here we will be safe". I told them that I could not stay, but would write a note saying that the house was mine and that everyone in it was under my protection. I wrote it in Russian, German and English, and signed my name with the Russian pass number underneath. I also gave them my Air Force insignia as proof that I had been there. I do not know how much, if any, this helped them, but it was all that I could do. They were grateful for any help.

In contrast to the act of brutality previously described, individual Russians could be generous and congenial toward others whom they considered friends. The few favorable memories that I have of red army men are those experienced with small groups on outpost duty. We were always away from the main army groups and thus they could relax and act as they wished. When not on duty we would gather around a campfire and talk about various subjects, all in a friendly relaxed manner. They would share what food they had which was very meager by American standards. A Russian soldier's ration for one day was three "baseball" size bread rolls which had to be toasted and soaked in thin soup to be eaten. They would stick them on a bayonet and hold them over the fire much like roasting a hot dog. I was offered half of this ration, but declined, because it was all that they had and I could get food from the Red Cross parcels at the P.O.W. camp.

There was one Ukrainian soldier whom I became friends with. He was well educated and interested in America. We conversed in German which he had studied in school. He said that German and English were compulsory in school and that students had to take one, or the other. It was interesting to get a first hand account of his life growing up in the Soviet Ukraine. It was not too different from a boy growing up anywhere and he was anxious to get back home and start life all over again. I asked him if he was a communist, he said no that he was not a member of the party, but that he believed in his country and supported his government. Fair enough, I would not have expected him to say otherwise.

Although individual Russians as stated above could be friendly and act decent on occasion, I never once saw one show any mercy to a German of any age, or sex. They were especially brutal to German P.O.W.'s which I thought was totally unnecessary that late in the war. They had one thing in mind as they swept across Germany—Revenge—and they took it out on anyone that they met.

Soon after these events, I was contacted by the commissar. A "commissar" is a political officer attached to all communist armies to insure that all soldiers adhere to the party line and remain "good" communists. I was at first apprehensive, not knowing what to expect. However, he quickly put me at ease by being in a friendly and conciliatory mood. He said in effect that they had checked me out and wished to make me an offer. He opened a dossier on his desk and proceeded to tell me all about myself. Where did he get the dossier? Then I remembered the one that the Germans used to interrogate me at Dulag Luft. He probably got it there. My mind at ease, I sat back and listened to what he had to say. He told me that since I had not graduated from college, that they would send me to Moscow and I could finish my education there. He also told me that I should tour the Soviet Union as their guest so I could become better acquainted with Russia. All that I had to do was sign some papers and I could start at once. I was stunned. Why did they want me? It was 1945 and they were our ally against the common enemy, but from what I had already seen, I knew that I did not like Russians. I did not know then anything about communism, or communists, but if they acted like Russians, then I wanted no part of it. I said no, thank you, I want to go home as soon as possible. He said to do that I would still have to sign some documents. I went back to the P.O.W. camp and checked with the senior officer about signing the documents. He said that he had checked with London and it was okay to sign them, that they were sort of a passport to get out of Soviet territory. I was flown out along with other P.O.W's in B-17's sent from England. I was finally on my way home.

While flying over Germany to France, I was startled to see the change that had taken place since I came through by train in April, 1944. Germany was totally devastated; the cities were bombed out ruins. I thought, could we have done all of this? It seemed incredible that a country could be so utterly destroyed. It was an awesome testimony to what air power can do. As we flew low over what had been the city of Cologne, I looked down with mixed emotions at the bombed out cathedral with its tall spire still pointing toward the sky from which all this death and destruction had come. Sherman was right, war is hell![41]

Summary

I was honorably discharged from active military service in September, 1945. I was 23 years old and had survived four years of war. I did not then, or now consider myself a "hero". I just did my duty. I am, however, proud of my combat record and doubt that anyone could have done much better. As for being shot down and captured, I will quote General Eisenhower in his speech to us in France on May 23, 1945. He said, "Speaking for everyone in America, I want to express our gratitude to you all in helping us defeat Germany. You men carried the ball for us and we will not forget it". I am proud of what I did for my country and hope that my grandchildren who read this are too.

---

[41] Quote from William Tecumseh Sherman – Union General during the American Civil War.

Chapter VII

Claude had a few of these stories written down, but the majority was written when my wife, Pamela, began work on a website for the memoirs in 2001. To incorporate them into the original memoir at this time, I felt, would take away from the flow of the previously written account. So, they are shown separately here. I have placed them in order as best I could.

It was not all bad – Some Humorous Incidents

Chewing Gum

On a secret one plane mission from Tunis in North Africa to Italy we landed at our airstrip at dusk. We taxied to the end of the runway and paused to contact headquarters. As the plane stopped rolling I was sitting in my nose compartment when suddenly a little Italian boy about ten years old climbed up the nose wheel and jumped in my lap! He very calmly asked, "Got some chewing gum Joe?" I was surprised and amazed! When I regained my composure, I asked him where he came from. He grinned and said, "I was waiting for planes to come in, I get lots of chewing gum that way." We called for a jeep to come get him and take him home. I wondered if his mother spanked him!

The moral of this incident to me was: "So much for secret missions if kids know about them!"

The Cigars

The day I was shot down and captured by the German Army, I was first put in a room in a house used as quarters by German Officers. I was assigned an orderly and told if I wanted anything to tell him. The orderly was a young teenage army private who spoke English. After getting over the surprise of being well treated and even respected by these particular Germans I decided to test this "if you want anything to ask." I called the orderly who came in and saluted then asked what I wanted. I said, "Go get me some cigars." He looked puzzled and repeated, "Cigars?" I said, "Cigars." He then looked thoughtful and said, "Only the Officers have cigars, I will have to go to their quarters and steal some." I said, "Do it and hurry up." He saluted and went out the door. Shortly he came back with four cigars. I then asked for a match to light up which he produced. He was pleased with himself and I was surprised that I had pulled the whole thing off.

My good fortune lasted but a few minutes as three German Officers came in. This time I stood at attention and saluted. A Major asked, "Where did you get those cigars?" I said, "I brought them from Italy." The orderly sighed with relief and I made a friend in the German Army!

The Cookies

My second day of captivity in Yugoslavia was in a stable being used as a jail. I was put in a small brick cell apart from the other prisoners who were captured Yugoslav partisans. Two times a day a young German soldier who spoke English brought me food of soup and bread. He was a handsome blond, blue eyed youth who looked as if he should be in high school instead of the Army. On his first visit he showed me a letter from a U.S. POW camp for captured Germans. It was post marked Jackson, MS. He asked if I knew where that was and said his Uncle was a POW there. Of course I told him that I knew where Jackson was and that the POW's were well treated. He was pleased, smiled and left. On his next visit that evening he looked heavier. On entering my cell he closed the door, set my soup bowl down and unbuttoned his jacket, then I saw why he looked heavier, his jacket was bulging with cookies! He smiled and handed me a double handful and said, "Eat them all now, I got them from the Officer's mess and if they find out it will go bad for me." I looked at those dry cookies and wondered how I could eat all of them without having something to wash them down. I said, "You will have to help me if I am to eat them all." So we started cramming cookies down. After the last one was down, we picked up the crumbs from the straw covered floor!

Think of it, here I am eating cookies with one of my German captors as fast as we can to keep him from getting caught feeding cookies from the Officer's table to the enemy! Fantastic!

Post Script: I asked him for his name and address so I could contact him after the war. He said, "No", if they found his name in my possession that he would be court-martialed (or worse). I have wondered many times if he survived the war and what happened to him if he did.

The Errol Flynn Episode

When flying combat I dressed well so if shot down I would have on my uniform with its U.S. insignia to identify me as an American Officer. When shot down over Yugoslavia and captured I also kept my military bearing and confidence in the face of the Germans. This worked so well that when I was finally united with other POW's to be shipped to Germany they thought that I was a German spy! They were already in a large truck that stopped to pick me up. When the truck arrived I was escorted to it by two German Officers who by their manner and talk did not treat me as the POW's in the truck. I thought they should if I too was a POW. Consequently, when I got in the truck they gave me the cold shoulder and would not speak to me. I realized what was wrong and tried to think how to convince them who I was. It had to be something distinctly American. Errol Flynn was the leading adventure Hollywood movie star at the time so as the truck was crossing a river bridge, I said in my best

Southern drawl, "If I were Errol Flynn I would knock the guard out, jump over the bridge into the river and swim back to Italy." They looked startled, then laughed and said. "No one but an American would know to say that, you are one of us!"

Ham and Eggs

On the long train ride to a POW camp in Germany from Yugoslavia where I was captured there were many stops. One such stop was in Vienna, Austria. We missed connections with the train that was to take us on into Germany so we spent most of the day waiting for the next one. The railroad station in Vienna was large and well furbished. It was comparable to any in the U.S. So I enjoyed watching the civilians come and go to the trains and to look around the spacious lobby. I could do this, because I was not "hand cuffed," or otherwise restrained. In fact except for my U.S. uniform, no one would have known that I was a captured enemy airman. I was traveling with two Luft Waffe Sergeants who were happy and in a good humor because they were going home on leave. Their sole duty was to deliver me to the POW interrogation center in Frankfurt.

While looking fascinated at American western novels by Zane Grey and Max Brand in a large book display case, I heard someone come up behind me and say, "Ham and eggs." I looked around and saw an elderly gentleman dressed in Austrian Tyrolean clothes complete with a feather on his hat. He smiled and said again, "Ham and eggs." I tried to talk to him, but got nowhere, so I called one of my bilingual guards and asked him to see what the gentleman wanted. After a brief conversation in German the guard said that "Ham and Eggs" was all the English that he knew, and that he had heard that all Americans ate ham and eggs and he wanted to say "Ham and Eggs" to the only American available which was me.

With the guard interpreting I enjoyed visiting with him and found out that he had relatives in the U.S. and that he liked America. In fact most all Austrian and Germans that I met liked Americans and did not understand why we were fighting them. It was not the time or place for me to try and explain why we were at war with Germany. I was just thankful that I was captured early in the war before they got "mad" at us.

Soap and Razor

After capture in Yugoslavia I was loaded on a train in Zagreb which would take us to Vienna, Austria. On arrival in Vienna our train was late and we missed the one to Germany. This meant a long layover and my two guards didn't want to sit and "guard" me all day until the train to Germany arrived, so we all went to a large canteen for German soldiers on leave. It was a huge place with hundreds of German soldiers coming and going. Food and refreshments were served by girl hostesses in pretty red and white uniforms. It was a cheerful place that made the war seem far away. The guards got us a table and after being served, got up and left telling me that I could go anywhere in the room, but not to leave it, or I would be shot! After observing the situation, I noticed soldiers with towels, soap and razors lined up before lavatories across the room. It had been almost a week since I was captured and I had not had a chance to wash, or shave so I was very dirty and "grubby". I thought a minute and decided to go get in line for a lavatory. I walked across the room, got in line and waited my turn. When I got to the lavatory I realized that I had neither soap, nor a razor. Without hesitating I tapped the shoulder of the German in front of me who had just finished and motioned that I would like to borrow his soap, razor and towel. I will never forget the look on his face when he turned and saw who had tapped him. It was a mixture of surprise and disbelief! He hesitated, then handed me his shaving equipment and towel. I used it, thanked him and handed it back as if nothing unusual had happened. The other soldiers around acted if nothing had happened. I went back to my table felling clean and refreshed, but in awe that I had gotten away with it, because a POW is just not supposed to act as brazen as I did!

For one to understand this you must realize that these were enemy soldiers on leave and thus in a good humor. That also, German soldiers understand and respect military courtesy, even though it is to a captured enemy officer. Any other time or place I could have been shot! The moral of the story is, a P.O.W. must know the mood of his captors and calculate what he can, or cannot get away with! On my part I looked and acted like an officer and kept a strict military bearing. I understood my status as a POW, but never acted sullen, or belligerent.

People often ask me, "How did the Germans treat you?" Never am I asked, "How did you treat the Germans?" In my opinion the answer to both questions is "mutual respect". The soap, razor and towel incident is an example.

The Button

During the long train ride from Yugoslavia where I was captured to Stalag Luft I POW camp in North Germany, many interesting incidents happened. The two German guards and I traveled by passenger coach along with the usual German civilians and soldiers going home on leave. I was not handcuffed, or otherwise restrained and was treated as if I were just another passenger. This gave me the opportunity to observe the German people and look at the countryside. I was surprised that I was treated so well and more of an object of curiosity than the hated enemy which I had been told would be the case.

I was wearing my flying officers uniform that I had been shot down in which had lots of buttons and insignia in plain sight. This attracted the attention of a small boy sitting with his mother across the aisle from me. He had been looking at me over the seat back and when he finally realized who I was he jumped out into the aisle, pointed his finger and shouted, "Amerikaner Flieger"! (American Flyer). I was the enemy! His mother tried to quiet him to no avail, finally she grabbed him by the arm and dragged him out of the coach still yelling, "Amerikaner Flieger!

The German soldiers were amused by all of this and one came over and pointed to my uniform buttons. He then asked in English if he could have one as a souvenir to take home to his little boy. He explained that he was going home on leave and that he wanted to impress his family. He added that they thought that he had been in combat when actually he worked in the headquarters' office far behind the front lines. He was very polite and a gentleman considering the fact that he could have taken the buttons from a P.O.W. I was impressed with him and the reason that he wanted the button, so I pulled off one of the large fold buttons with the embossed eagle upon it and added the wings and propeller insignia from my collar. He smiled and thanked me cordially. I wished him luck and said I hoped the American souvenirs got the desired results and that his little boy was duly impressed.

I was impressed with the human side of the enemy and was thankful that I was captured by Germans and not the Japanese.

Wahoo

While attending a recent Indian Pow-Wow[42], I remembered an Indian that I knew while a P.O.W. in Stalag Luft I at Barth, Germany. Of the many thousands of American P.O.W.'s in my compound there was one full blood Indian P.O.W. He was a handsome young man with dark skin and wore his black hair a little longer than most of us. He had a pleasant personality and we all liked him, but he was pretty

---

[42] An American Indian social gathering.

much a loner and kept mostly to himself. We never knew his real name so we called him "Wahoo" which he did not seem to mind.

Wahoo would go off to himself and make arrowheads out of glass then trade them to the German guards for food. Since food was always in short supply, Wahoo did pretty well for himself. Every effort to get him to show us how to make arrowheads failed. He would smile and say in effect, "That is my secret and one advantage of being Indian".

Wahoo's luck ran out when the Germans decided to separate the Jewish POW's from the rest of us. The Germans thought that Wahoo looked like a Jew so he must be a Jew. Wahoo was shocked and indignant that he the only true American in Stalag Luft I was being classified as someone whom he was not. He came to our room worried and angry that he would be sent off with the Jewish American P.O.W.'s to a concentration camp. He asked that we help him convince the Germans that he was an American Indian and not a Jew. After much arguing and explaining to the Germans just who Wahoo was they finally admitted their mistake and Wahoo stayed with us until war's end.

The happy ending to all of this was that even though the Jewish Americans were put in a barrack by themselves they were not mistreated, or taken from Stalag Luft I. As far as Wahoo was concerned the real injustice was not being recognized as an "Indian", the only Native American in the camp!

The Photograph

In May of 1945, I had just been liberated from Stalag Luft I prisoner of war camp near Barth, Germany by the Russian army. I was a member of a POW unit called the "Field Force" whose initial purpose was to contact the Russians then to work with them to insure the welfare of the 9,000 plus POW's in Stalag Luft I.

I was with a group of Russians who had just looted the headquarters of a German air base that I found a photograph of a German Officer that they had been torn from the wall, wadded up and thrown down. I picked it up, straightened it out and could tell by the uniform that he was a Captain in the Luftwaffe (air weapon). I had no idea who he was, but felt compelled to save the photo.

On arrival back at the POW camp I put it in my war time log book along with other photos and mementos. There it stayed until 1985 when I made slides of the log book photos to show to college military history classes. In 1999 I showed the slides once more at a Rotary International Club meeting in which a military historian was present. His special interest was the German Luftwaffe and he immediately recognized the photo as that of Hauptman (Captain) Wulf Dietrich Wilcke who was killed in action 20 April 1944. Now I not only had a name to go with the photo, but also knew his fate. I was to learn much more about the man in the photo. In July 2000 I purchased a book at the Barksdale AFB PX[43] on the Luftwaffe in North Africa, Italy and the Balkans where I flew missions as a Bombardier in the 15th AAF[44].

When I opened the book I was astonished to see the name of Wulf Dietrich Wilcke as one of the leading aces of JG53 with 34 confirmed kills in North Africa and Italy and before he was "KIA" ran his score of allied planes shot down to 161! One of which could very well have been my B-24 bomber shot down 2 April 1944!

Never in my wildest dreams would I have ever thought that day in May 1945 when I picked up that photo that over 50 years later I would learn so much of the wartime history of the man in it. Some would call it an odd coincidence, I call it a miracle! I "salute" Hauptman Wulf Dietrich Wilcke, because although we were on opposite sides in WWII, fate brought us together through that photo picked up at Barth, Germany in May 1945!

---

[43] Acronym for Post Exchange – a store where various items are for sell.
[44] Acronym for Army Air Force.

Conclusion

As noted in the text, Claude returned home in September of 1945 and settled down in Shreveport, Louisiana with his wife Marilynn. With war reparation money received from Germany he built a house he still lives in at the time of this writing.

Shortly after the war, he became a cattle buyer for a packing plant in Shreveport. He traveled over a five state area purchasing cattle never being able to settle down to a desk job, though offered many times by the various companies he worked for. The confinement of the prison camp still hung over him and he enjoyed and felt comfort in the open air and freedom of travel.

Claude flew with the reserves at Barksdale Air Force Base until the Korean War. He was asked to become active again, but his wife could not let her husband march off to another war. Obeying her wishes, he remained at home and reluctantly let go of military life.

He began to recount his experiences to audiences after being asked by cadets of the Centenary College[45] Reserve Officer Training Corp in the middle 1980's. An excerpt from this speech can be viewed on the last page of this memoir.

While recounting his experience helped at first, the haunting of what he had done and seen began to become ever stronger. Never shrinking away from anything he felt compelled to do, he continued to recount his story and especially felt satisfaction when sharing his experience with airmen of the modern air force, most of whom, have benefited from his knowledge.

Like so many veterans, the demons of war never fully let go, and the war continues in the mind. Claude received a

---

[45] Located in Shreveport, LA

100% disability pension from the Veteran's Administration for the experiences he encountered during the war.

He retired from cattle buying in the early eighties and took up archaeology as a hobby. Today, he is a well respected avocational archaeologist in three states having found and documented well over 600 sites with the help of his field secretary Ruth Rainey. He is fully retired now and spends his time between home and facilities at Barksdale Air Force Base located in Bossier City, Louisiana.

This is one story of many that has been told of the war. Many fought in it and have never fully shared their experience. It is sad that history is lost in this manner when it could be shared and helpful to future generations, especially for those who may, someday, find themselves in a similar situation and, having learned from such shared knowledge, discovered something that may save their life or make their experience less traumatic. It is our hope that the reader has found this memoir informative and educational.

References

Turner Publishing Company

1994   456th Bomb Group 1943-1945 Steed's Flying Colts
       ISBN: 1-56311-141-1

Robert F. Dorr

2000   B-24 Liberator Units of the Fifteenth Air force ISBN:
       1-84176-081-1

War Status of the Flight Crew of "Miss Zeke"[47] A/C #42-52276

Lt. William Terrell - POW[48] Stalag Luft 1
Lt. Phillip Crum - POW Stalag Luft 1
F/O Seymor Stutzel – POW Stalag Luft 1
F/O Claude McCrocklin - POW Stalag Luft 1
Sgt. Palmer Lerum – KIA[49]
Sgt. Dennis King – KIA
Sgt. Herman Lipkin - Evadee
Sgt. Chester Eide - POW Stalag Luft 17B
Sgt. Charles Doerring – POW Stalag Luft 17B
Sgt. Warren Stuckey - Evadee

Sgt. Warren Stuckey received the Distinguished Flying Cross for saving the lives of two crew members and evading the enemy on the ground.

After being wounded by flak, Sgt. Stuckey un-jammed the ball turret, extracted Sgt. Eide from it, so he could bail out. He also placed tourniquets on the leg of Sgt. Lerum, the tail gunner, whose leg had been shot off above the knee, and pushed him from the aircraft. Sgt. Lerum later died on the ground from his wounds.

Sgt. Stuckey was able to join a group of Yugoslav Partisans and successfully evade the German patrols eventually returning to the 456th BG base at Cerignola, Italy.

---

[47] The original B-24 assigned to the crew at Davis Montham Army Air Base in Tuscon, Arizona, was named "Nita-Lynn" after the pilot's, William Terrell, wife Anita and Claude's wife Marilynn. Upon arrival in North Africa, the "Nita-Lynn" was confiscated by a general (because it was a new plane) and the crew was then assigned to the war-weary "Miss Zeke."
[48] POW – Prisoner of War
[49] KIA – Killed In Action

Close friends before the war, Claude arranged to have Warren Stuckey placed on the same crew as himself (at the request of Warren's sister – whom Claude dated in Overton, Texas before the war). Pictured above are Warren Stuckey (left) and Claude McCrocklin (right) in the fall of 1990.

Claude W. McCrocklin - Fact sheet

Dates: Called to active duty – 1/26/43, US departure date – 2/7/44, Arrival date to base of operations – 2/23/44, European departure date – 6/16/45, US arrival date – 6/21/45, Release from active duty 9/45

Service: Continuous service – 10 months 23 days, Foreign Service – 14 months 5 days

Total combat time: 59 hours 30 minutes

Training Locations: Preflight School – Santa Ana, CA, Advanced Bombardier School – Deming AFB, Deming, New Mexico

Medals: Air Medal with one oak leaf cluster; Campaign Medal with three bronze stars

Theatres of War: European, African, Middle Eastern

Missions:

1 - 3/3/44 – Viterbo Landing Area No. 2 North of Rome
2 - 3/4/44 – Dresden, Germany (cancelled due to bad weather)
3 - 3/7/44 - Viterbo Landing Area No. 2 North of Rome
4 - 3/15/44 – Cassino, Italy (Monte Cassino)
5 - 3/15/44 – Aquino, Italy (bad weather forced return)
6 - 3/17/44 – Vienna, Austria
7 - 3/18/44 – Maniago, Italy
8 - 3/19/44 – Steyr, Austria – bombed alternate target of Klagenfurt, Austria
9 - 3/22/44 – Rimini and Bologna, Italy
10 - 3/26/44 – Steyr, Austria – bombed alternate target of Maniago, Italy
11 - 3/29/44 – Milan Lambrate-Serriate, Italy
12 - 4/2/44 – Steyr, Austria (shot down this mission)

Claude W. McCrocklin August, 2008

Prisoner of War Recognition Day - Barksdale Air Force Base

Excerpt from a 1985 speech given to the Centenary College R.O.T.C (Reserve Officer Training Corp) students:

I welcome this opportunity to share with you some of my experiences during World War II. This Great War which so affected the course of history and created the problems with communism with which we are confronted today was the last war which our nation went all out to win. To those of us who fought in World War II, it is as fresh in our mind as if it happened only yesterday. Combat soldiers who are in direct contact with the enemy for long periods of time don't forget they only learn to live with it. I still have bad dreams and think about many of my experiences. I wish that I could forget, but I can hardly turn on the TV, or read the paper without seeing something about World War II. By the time that I was 22 years old, I had been through so

much that everything that happened since has seemed like an anti-climax. It has been hard to adjust to a normal life ever since. I am proud of you in the R.O.T.C. By being in the R.O.T.C., you have demonstrated an interest in keeping your country strong and perhaps a career in the Armed Forces. For whatever the reason, wear your uniform proudly, because civilian soldiers such as you have kept our country strong for the past 200 years.